**Jane Jurkscheit**

I0752425

# An analysis of the success factors in implementing an ITIL-based IT Change and Release Management Application

## Based on the IBM Change and Configuration Management Database (CCMDB)

Anchor Academic Publishing

**Jurkscheit, Jane: An analysis of the success factors in implementing an ITIL-based IT Change and Release Management Application: Based on the IBM Change and Configuration Management Database (CCMDB). Hamburg, Anchor Academic Publishing 2013**

Buch-ISBN: 978-3-95489-072-9
PDF-eBook-ISBN: 978-3-95489-572-4
Druck/Herstellung: Anchor Academic Publishing, Hamburg, 2013

**Bibliografische Information der Deutschen Nationalbibliothek:**
Die Deutsche Nationalbibliothek verzeichnet diese Publikation in der Deutschen Nationalbibliografie; detaillierte bibliografische Daten sind im Internet über http://dnb.d-nb.de abrufbar.

**Bibliographical Information of the German National Library:**
The German National Library lists this publication in the German National Bibliography. Detailed bibliographic data can be found at: http://dnb.d-nb.de

## I Abstract

To ensure the quality of the IT environment for the future the majority of IT managers followed a strategy to introduce an IT change and release management application in the past few years. The present book researches if the implementations of the given success factors are leading to a successful implementation of a workflow-based IT change and release management application and will moreover find further success factors. This is done with help of five hypothesises. The five hypothesises are based on the HR change management issues, on the ITIL® reference model and on general process issues.

The HR change management offers with the eight step model of Kotter critical success factor for changes in the business. Publications of Kotter are used to illustrate that the described success factors lead to successful HR change implementation. The ITIL® reference model defines critical success factors for a successful IT change and release management implementation and are used for a research study for the effectiveness of this model. The ITIL® reference model and process issues publications of the official ITIL® source and literature of Laudon & Laudon are used for the present book. In addition other researchers in this field are important mentioned as well.

Subsequent to that, the findings were integrated into the questionnaire and the interviews and used as well get an initial assessment. The mixture of the qualitative and quantitative approaches uses the strengths of both methods. The given answers strongly depend on the respondent's point of view.

It becomes clear that a successful implementation of an IT change and release management application comes not only from the implementation of the HR change management issues but also from the implementation of the IT issues. The combination of HR and IT issues with their specialised success factors is the best way to gain a successful IT change and release management implementation. But the research discovered further improvements and optimisations which mainly deal with redesigned processes.

The process redesigns based on modification on the ITIL® reference model to optimise the IT change process. The optimisations include a skip of the formal RfC request form to shorten the whole process-chain during the application of an IT change. Furthermore an implementation of a key technical employee should be deploy to authorise the IT change instead of an authorisation of the central positioned change manager.

The recommendations at the end of this research study are helpful for the Anonym-IT GmbH organisation as well as for other companies. Theoretical implications could be done as well for the ITIL® reference model and for MIS implementation success factors.

**Table of contents**

## List of figures and graphs



## II List of tables

## Glossary and Abbreviations

| | |
|---|---|
| BPR | Business Process Reengineering |
| CCMDB | Change and Configuration Management Database |
| CI | Configuration Item |
| CIO | Chief Information Officer |
| CCMDB | Change and Configuration Management Database |
| CMDB | Configuration Management Database |
| COBIT | Control Objectives for Information and Related Technology |
| DB | Database |
| HR | Human Resource |
| IEC | International Electro-technical Commission |
| IS | Information System |
| ISO | International Organization for Standardization |
| IT | Informations Technology |
| ITIL | IT Infrastructure Library |
| ITSM | IT Service Management |
| KPI | Key Performance Indicator |
| MIS | Management Information System |
| RfC | Request for Change |
| TQM | Total Quality Management |

# 1. Introduction

This introduction contains a summarisation of the organisation that explaining how it is structured and the linked between the main departments. The following chapter contains a description of the course of the IT change and release management application project which is the basis for the research of the present book. The third part of the introduction defines the aims and illustrates the demarcation. Finally the procedures chapter gives an overview of the structure.

## 1.1. The organisation

This chapter starts with the description of the Anonym group and their subordinate company Anonym-IT GmbH which is responsible for the IT infrastructure.

### 1.1.1. The Anonym group

The Anonym group is the umbrella organisation which contains many subordinate companies. The Anonym group one of the leading retail, travel and tourism companies in Europe.

### 1.1.2. The Anonym-IT GmbH

Anonym-IT GmbH is the central and international solution provider for the information- and telecommunication systems. The Anonym-IT GmbH was established in 1991 as an independent company inside of the Anonym-IT Group.

Today the Anonym-IT GmbH has more than 750 IT-specialists mainly based in Cologne. The main purpose of the company is to modernise and optimise existing systems and find ways to make IT more efficient for the company as a whole. They set the standards for IT- assignment for the retailing business and develops new technologies for the trade sector.

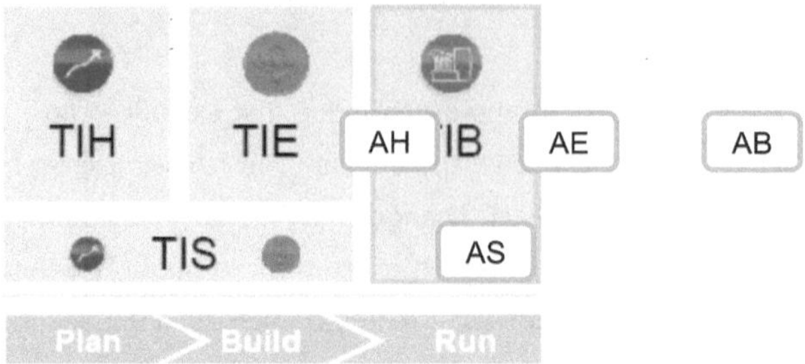


The Anonym-IT GmbH uses the operative (run), tactical (build) and strategically (plan) model. It is a circular life-cycle with distinct steps where each stage has a cascading effect on the other.

The operational area is the AB unit and contains mainly IT administrators which are on a daily basis responsible for an error free operation of all the servers and applications of the Anonym-IT GmbH inclusive with 24x7 on-call support.

Nearly 300 IT administrators are working in AB and they are nationwide in charge of over 1,500 server systems inclusive storage libraries, 13,500 network connections, 10,000 scanner terminals in the shops and much more. The AB unit is also responsible for the IT change and release management application implementation, located in the department ABX.

## 1.2. Course of the project

IT is described as an enabler for the business but the ever increasing IT infrastructure with its ever increasing complexity has become its own challenge for the Anonym-IT GmbH as well as for other companies.

The IT environment has in the last 10 years grown extremely fast and many companies were not able to adapt to the fast pace of the IT infrastructure and the restructuring needed to organise the work of the IT administrators properly. To ensure the quality of the IT environment for the future the majority of IT managers have followed a strategy to introduce an IT change and release management application in the past few years.

Anonym-IT GmbH introduced in year 2006 a web-based non-process IT change management form named Wikie without including any type of workflows or processing issues. IT administrators had to fill out forms with some required information to open an IT change and did not get any important or additional feedback from the system.

About two years later two independent external IT consulting companies, discovered in year 2008 the missing process-controlled IT change and release management application and the management of Anonym-IT GmbH decided to implement such an application where the production stated goal should be reached the end of the year 2009. The project started 2008 with an evaluation of the available CMDB tools on the market and the decision was made for IBM's Chance and Configuration Management Database (CCMDB) application where the surface interfaces and workflows could be modified for the special needs of Anonym-IT GmbH.

At the same time some internal workshops were generated to work out the needs and requirements for the IT change and release management application implementation inclusive their inputs of operational sequences and requirements for the workflow as well as the process design.

Two months later the top management of the company decided to generate a productive project group with seven employees who were in the position to realise the implementation of the IT change and release management. It was a preliminary stage before the business unit IT Service Management department unit was generated.

The reason for the series of workshops was that inside of the company there were no defined and documented processes which could be mapped one to one into the CCMDB application. The missing processes on paper made optimisation and evaluation of the processes nearly impossible and had to be collected first from every expertise team. The employees are working mostly together on call for years which of course can be seen as a kind of process but it is not an overall defined and standardised process for a structural work for the whole workforce inside of the Anonym-IT GmbH company.

The result of the workshops was a huge amount of processes which were implemented into the IT change and release management application. With these complicated processes, technical discrepancies and problems within management it was easy for the employees to avoid as well as to resist the new IT change and release management application. After two month of being online with the application it was became clear for every one involved that a positive impact was not viewed and a continuation of the rollout had to be stopped for the time being.

The management of Anonym-IT GmbH agreed to a second attempt to implement the IT change and release management application without repeating past mistakes. The managers implemented organisational changes and the ITSM team was in the position to redesign the application usage.

It was a challenge for the second attempt to deal with the environmental change and introduction of the IT change and release management application at the same time. These reason being was that the internal working system and the social networking between the employees were changing significantly.

This circumstance which had to be respected in another way compared to the initial position of the first attempt of the rollout. For the second attempt at the IT change and release management application implementation a series of small workshop with less than 10 employees of the department unit AB were held before the process and the surface of the application was redesigned. In this phase a decision was made that the ITIL® v3 reference model should support the new process design.

The second implementation started in the end of September 2011 with the first department inside of the AB unit and was finished in the middle of March with the last department in the whole AB unit.

### 1.3. Aims

The aim of this present research study is to analyse the success factors of an implementation of an IT change and release management application in the operational AB unit of the organisation.

To measure success the word itself has to be described and defined. Therefore an evaluation of key success factors had to be set. With a measurement tool the success can be analysed and interpreted for both implementation attempts.

An implementation of an IT change and release management application involves organisational human resources, IT specific and process issues. The non-process web form and the both attempts of the rollout of the application will be analysed as well as compared. The result will be able to show that the described success factors given in the process / literature had a positive effect in implementation of an IT change and release management application. Furthermore the result should be able to find issues to improve the implemented IT change and release management application which could not be found in the process / literature to improve the project in the long-term existence.

From the management perspective the recommendations of the present research study were able to improve the IT change and release management application implementation.

The improvements led to a higher positive return of investment, leading to a more effective IT service management, improving of business services and a standardisation the processes reaching a higher quality of service for the Anonym-IT GmbH organisation as well for other companies.

The data collection needed for the approach is further defined and described in chapter 3.

## 1.4. Demarcation

In the past few years many IT change and release management applications were introduced on the market and these have individual strengths and weaknesses for every organisation. Every organisation is in the position to figure out which application is the right one for their needs and this research study will not call into question the CCMDB application. Moreover this book will not describe the technical problems and issues which can occur or occurred during an implementation of an IT change management application. For this there is enough more specialised literature and expertise knowledge available and thus it is not a subject of this research study.

Additionally the present book will not deal with the risks and financial issues inclusive in a profitability analysis. The decision to implement an IT change and release management application was made from the management and will not contested or justified.

The focus of this research study is on the conceptually part of the implementation of an IT change management application with the involvement of the human resource change management and IT change and release management process issues.

## 1.5. Procedure

The present book is structured into the following chapters:

- Chapter 2: Contains a theoretical review of the research which described the existing approaches for a successful implementation of an organisational change as well as success factor of the implementation of an IT change and release management application.
- Chapter 3: Explains the chosen methodology for primary data research.
- Chapter 4: Presents the results of chapter 3 and analysis of these questionnaires and interviews.
- Chapter 5: Conclusions of the research findings and as well as an explanation of the theoretical implications.

Figure 1 illustrates the structure of the book.

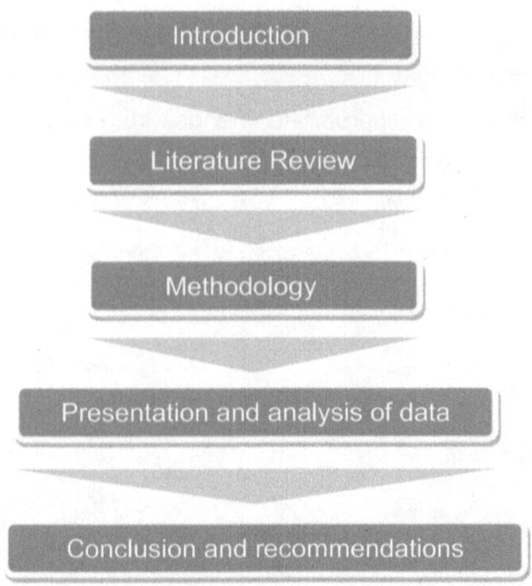


**Figure 1: Illustration of the structureofft resarœh study (Own diagram)**

## 2. Literature Review

To have an effectively run business the Anonym-IT GmbH company the employees have to perform effectively. If the managers of a business decides to change or modify in-company issues the employees are naturally affected. Not every employee is able to acclimate to these changes and can resist, becoming demotivated or there can occur other reasons which decrease the overall efficiency. Human resource change management strategies were implemented in the past few decades to motivate as well as to avoid a reduction of the efficiency of the employees and therefore for the business.

The employees are not the only enabler for the business but also the role of the IT infrastructure become more important in the last years. The IT becomes an important supporter for the business with their IT-based automatised processes which are able to increase the efficiency of every organisation.

While IT has been seen primarily as a rationalisation tool in the early days, it is increasingly viewed as an important competitive factor for organisations (Tiemeyer, 2011). Additionally, the value contribution of IT to business success is discussed (keyword: "IT Governance") today (Tiemeyer, 2011). With the changing role of IT in businesses there are, of course, appropriate changes in the requirements of modern IT management (Tiemeyer, 2011).

## 1.5. Procedure

The present book is structured into the following chapters:

- Chapter 2: Contains a theoretical review of the research which described the existing approaches for a successful implementation of an organisational change as well as success factor of the implementation of an IT change and release management application.
- Chapter 3: Explains the chosen methodology for primary data research.
- Chapter 4: Presents the results of chapter 3 and analysis of these questionnaires and interviews.
- Chapter 5: Conclusions of the research findings and as well as an explanation of the theoretical implications.

Figure 1 illustrates the structure of the book.

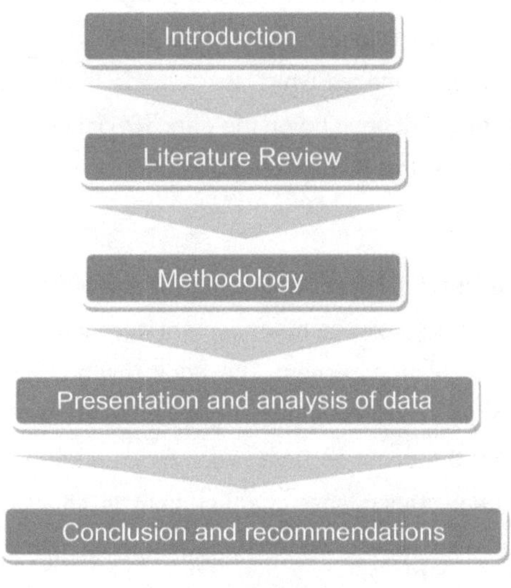


**Figure 1: Illustration of the structure oft resarcch study (Own diagram)**

Thus it roughly is comprehensible that 2/3 of the IT implementations have failed in the past years because not every company is able to go as far as should be necessary. Another reason for the high failure rate is due to underestimation of the human and organisational issues. The reason depends on the complexity of the relationship between organisational change and the IT systems (Lientz & Rea, 2004). "Persistent and lasting change is often best supported through automation; getting results from investment in IT often requires change in the work and processes." (Lientz & Rea, 2004)

Because of the ever increasing IT environments, especially in larger companies, the role of IT inevitably got their own strategy for the IT landscapes. To embrace the IT strategy new departments with IT leaders named Chief Information Officer (CIO) were created. CIO's have also to be efficient with their IT environments to support the efficiency of the organisation. To control the workforce and the modification on IT components an IT change and release management was implemented in a number of companies especially in larger organisations.

A result of the implementation of a workflow-based and process orientated IT change and release management application inclusive to their introduction affected the employees as well like other changes which were made in an organisation. The IT strategy is like the business is depending on the effective attitude towards the work of the employees and therefore the human resource change management issues are involved as well.

It is obvious that a successful implementation of management information (MIS) system, like the IT change and release management application is, will have to deal with technical and behaviour approaches. The book researches the impact of the implementation as a means to understand changes for the organisation as well as for the employees. To reach the common goal in an common infrastructure the implementation of an IT change and release management is affected by the following summarised key issues which have to be respected for the a successful realisation:

- Critical success factors of organisational change management
- Critical success factors of an IT system implementation
- IT process modelling with the support of a reference models

## 1.5. Procedure

The present book is structured into the following chapters:

- Chapter 2: Contains a theoretical review of the research which described the existing approaches for a successful implementation of an organisational change as well as success factor of the implementation of an IT change and release management application.
- Chapter 3: Explains the chosen methodology for primary data research.
- Chapter 4: Presents the results of chapter 3 and analysis of these questionnaires and interviews.
- Chapter 5: Conclusions of the research findings and as well as an explanation of the theoretical implications.

Figure 1 illustrates the structure of the book.

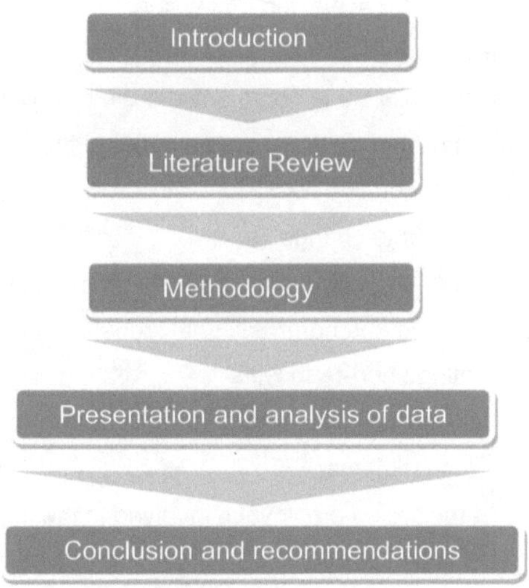


**Figure 1: Illustration of the structure of th researœh study (Own diagram)**

the realisation of new strategies, structures, systems, processes and / or behaviours which should be implement into the organisation.

Kotter (1996) says that a change process in an organisation goes through a series of phases which needs a considerable length of time. Skipping a phase creates the illusion of quickness but the quality of the change is not given as a result (Kotter, 1996). Kotter (1996) developed the eight steps model to increase the chance to lead an organisation to success:

1. Establishing a sense of urgency
    - Examining market and competitive realities
    - Identifying and discussing crises, potential crises, or major opportunities
2. Forming a powerful guiding coalition
    - Assembling a group with enough power to lead the change effort
    - Encouraging the group to work together as a team
3. Creating a vision
    - Creating a vision to help direct the change effort
    - Developing strategies for achieving that vision
4. Communicating the vision
    - Using every vehicle possible to communicate the new vision and strategies
    - Teaching new behaviours by the example of the guiding coalition
5. Empowering others to act on the vision
    - Getting rid of obstacles to change
    - Changing systems or structures that seriously undermine the vision
    - Encouraging risk taking and non-traditional ideas, activities, and actions
6. Planning for and creating short-term wins
    - Planning for visible performance improvements
    - Creating those improvements
    - Recognising and rewarding employees involved in the improvements

7. Consolidating improvements and producing still more change
   - Using increased credibility to change systems, structures, and policies that do not fit the vision
   - Hiring, promoting, and developing employees who can implement the vision
   - Reinvigorating the process with new projects, themes, and change agents
8. Institutionalising new approaches
   - Articulating the connections between new behaviours and corporate success
   - Developing the means to ensure leadership development and succession

One of the key issue during the change is the communication which is further defined in the kind of communication, the time, the content and the target group of to be informed persons (Balogun & Hailey, 2008). These issues embedded into the eight steps model of Kotter lead to a holistic overview of the model which it can be seen in the following figure 3.

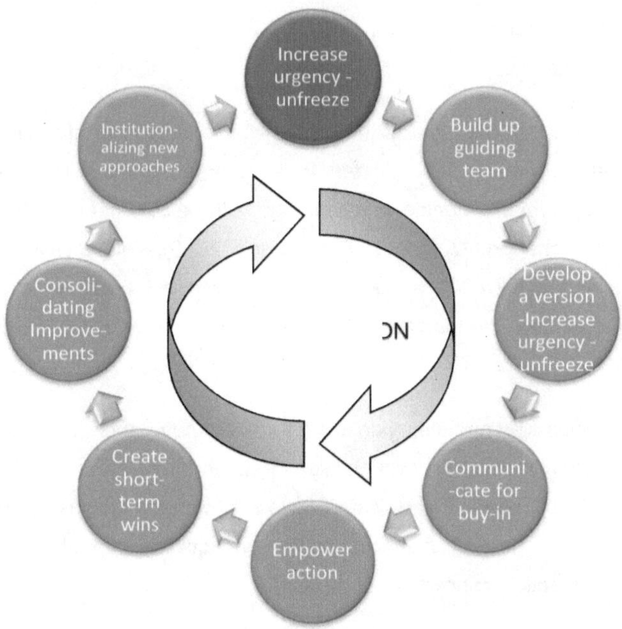


**Figure 3: Eight step model for HR change management (Adapted from Kotter, 1996)**

The usage of the eight steps model is not automatically a guarantee for a success. It is more a guidance for those issues which should be respected during a change management process.

As logical the eight steps model from Kotter seems to be but it is, like other models also given in the literature it is still affected by challenges and mistakes which are made during the change management processes in an organisation.

One of the biggest challenge is the emotional factors on people attitudes to change (Haberberg & Rieple, 2008). Kotter and Schlesinger (2008) said that resistance of change is because of the misunderstanding and lack of trust. If people in demanding situations retreat into familiar, and thus psychologically comfortable, territory, they make conservative decisions (Haberberg & Rieple, 2008). Potential triggers for this include (Haberberg & Rieple, 2008):

- Fear of the new
- Loss of autonomy
- Fear of incompetence
- Change fatigue

Another challenge is that the most of the organisations have a lot of small and large changes running at the same time (Anderson & Anderson, 2010). This fact makes it difficult for the employees to decide which change is the most important and it seems that they resist the changes (Anderson & Anderson, 2010). This is NOT an issue of the employees and is therefore a leadership issue where the management has to make the changes understandable for all involved (Anderson & Anderson, 2010).

A lack of the vision is also a challenging issue for many companies which are helping to clarify the direction in which an organisation needs to move (Kotter, 1996). Without having a well-defined and communicated vision, a transforming effort can easily dissolve into a list of confusing and incompaABle projects that can take the organisation in the wrong direction or nowhere at all (Kotter, 1996).

A change needs clear and thoughtful governance with a clear structure of the roles that are needed to lead and carry out the change (Anderson & Anderson, 2010). If managers delegate the plan of action to the project team they must not forget to give them authority to making key decisions (Anderson & Anderson, 2010).

Most people have not the patience to support a long-term change and want to see the first result between 12 and 24 months (Kotter, 1996). Without having some short-term achievement the majority of people may join the ranks of those who have been resisting the change or simply give up (Kotter, 1996).

Capacity is often underestimated and leaders are loading changes on the top of their everyday operational work which leads to stress, a drop in morale and lowed performance (Anderson & Anderson, 2010). The timeline of changes must be defined as well as the maintenance of the operational performance without over-burdening people (Anderson & Anderson, 2010).

Prokesch (2009) offers for the company General Electric a not "real" formula to interpret the effectiveness of a change. He said that the acceptance of change multiplied with the quality of the analysis is the result of an effectiveness change. If one of the factors is null the result is similarly null.

## 2.3. Critical success factors of an IT system implementation

Beyond the success factors of the change management the introduction of an IT involves much more than new software and hardware (Laudon & Laudon, 2012).

First of all the impact of the new IT system should clearly determine the organisational change. Laudon & Laudon categorise four common forms as follow:

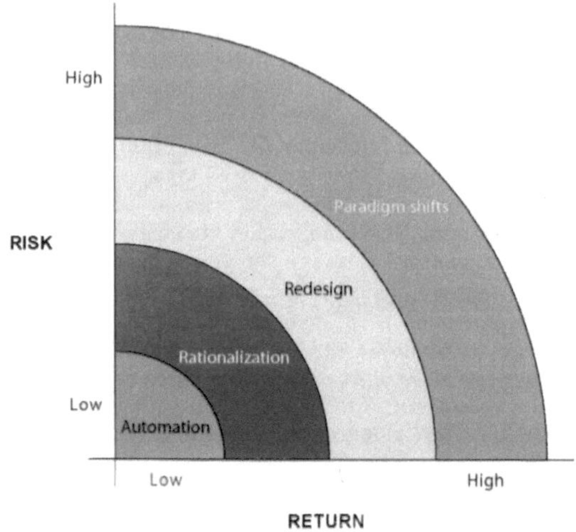


**Figure 4: Organisational change carries risks and rewards (Laudon & Laudon, 2012)**

The implementation of an IT change and release management is one of the paradigm shifts because it involves rethinking the nature of the business and the nature of the organisation (Laudon & Laudon, 2012). Paradigm shifts is very difficult to orchestrate and have often failed (Laudon & Laudon, 2012). One of the main challenges for a paradigm shift is the transformation of the business processes into the IT system.

A process, according to Davenport (1993) is "a structured, measured set of activities designed to produce a specified output for a particular customer or market. It implies a strong emphasis on how work is done within an organisation".

### 2.3.1. Business process reengineering

In terms of the IT change and release management processes a business process reengineering (BPR) is to implement which "builds on total quality management (TQM) and therefore business process reengineering is further defined to illustrate the key components of reengineering, fundamental thinking, radical redesign, processes and dramatic improvements." (Suhendra & Oswari, 2011)

The BPR methodology is may be characterised from several definitions which three of them are listed in the Table 1.

| Davernport proposed the following steps | Jacobson et al. intended for BPR | The suggested methodology by Manganelli |
|---|---|---|
| (1) Identify processes for innovation;<br>(2) Identify change layers;<br>(3) Develop process visions;<br>(4) Understand existing processes;<br>(5) Design and prototype the new process;<br>(6) Identify processes for innovation;<br>(7) Identify change layers;<br>(8) Develop process visions;<br>(9) Understand existing processes;<br>(10) Design and prototype the new process. | (1) Develop business vision;<br>(2) Understand the existing business;<br>(3) Design the new business;<br>(4) Install the new business. | (1) Preparation: Organize the project team;<br>(2) Identification: Develop a customer-oriented process model;<br>(3) Vision: Select processes and formulate redesign opportunities;<br>(4) Solution: Define technical and organization requirements for the new process;<br>(5) Transformation: Implement the reengineering plan. |

**Table 1: BPR methodology (Adapted from Davenport, 1993b; Jacobson et al., 1995; Manganelli, 1993)**

To achieve higher profits and cost reduction, improve quality and productivity, and better customer service a successful reengineering project should include the following issues (Attaran & Wood, 1999):

1. Strategic alignment with the organisations strategic direction
2. Compelling business case for business change with measurable objectives
3. Proven methodology
4. Effective change management that addresses cultural transformation
5. Line management ownership and accountability
6. Knowledgeable and competent reengineering teams

With a failure rate of 70 per cent for BPR projects a survey was performed about the experience of Fortune 500 companies and large British companies to find out the following reasons according to Peltu, Clegg and Sell (1996) and Choi and Chan (1997):

1. Unclear concepts - too many terms and definitions as well as the misuse of terms
2. Pursuing a restructuring or downsising strategy rather than a reengineering approach
3. Lack of well-established methodology - problems with redesigned methods and approaches
4. Unrealistic expectations
5. Misinterpretation of BPR
6. Skills and resource shortages
7. Resistance and lack of top management commitment
8. Fear of downward decision making authority
9. The best people not seconded or dedicated on BPR design teams
10. Lack of corporate information systems and inadequate attention to providing appropriate new IT-based business systems
11. Incorrect objectives, scope and process selection - reengineering the wrong processes, without
12. Sufficient process improvement
13. Incapable of recognising the benefits of BPR

The process design must be transparent for the end users to ensure that the system reflects their business priorities and Informations needs (Laudon & Laudon, 2012). Moreover the transparency and understanding of the process decreases resistance of the employees which in turn can lead to more suggestions for improvements.

### 2.3.2. Additional success factors for IT systems

According to Laudon & Laudon (2012) the role of the end users is to be respected. To improve the success some additional specifications should be consider for the implementation of an IT system.

The usability and design of the IT system surface should be easy to learn and should not be that complicated as well as time-consuming more than it necessary must be (Laudon & Laudon, 2012).

Further factors are a good documentation, a well-defined training, security, support, system stability, clear defined roles and responsibilities, qualified project leaders and project management and reporting for and of the IT system (Laudon & Laudon, 2012).

## 2.4. IT process modelling with the support of a reference models

Every competitive organisation needs more or less the support of an IT environment and therefore has to establish the best usage of IT standards and practices which can be suited to its individual requirements (Năstase, 2009). A reference model has the advantage that the IT environment with their dependencies and jargons of all the IT components makes it transparent for everyone.

"The growing adoption of IT best practices has been driven by a requirement for the IT industry to better manage the quality and reliability of IT in business and to respond to a growing number of regulatory and contractual requirements." (Năstase, 2009)

A multitude of standards exists which can be applied to the IT systems and it is a challenge to figure out the best reference model for the current IT environment to satisfy their needs.

Three specific practices and standards reference model are becoming widely adopted around the world (Năstase, 2009):

- ITIL® v3
  Published by the UK Government to provide a best practice framework for IT service management.

- COBIT 4.1
  Published by ITGI and positioned as a high-level governance and control framework

- ISO/IEC 27002:2005
  Published by the International Organisation for Standardization (ISO) and International Electro-technical Commission (IEC) and derived from the UK Government's BS 7799, renamed ISO/IEC 17799:2005 to provide a framework of a standard for information security management.

### 2.4.1. Comparison of the three reference models

| AREA \ STAND | COBIT | ITIL | ISO27002 |
|---|---|---|---|
| **Function** | Mapping IT Process | Mapping IT Service Level Management | Information Security Framework |
| **Area** | 34 Processes and 4 Domains | 9 Processes | 10 Domains |
| **Issuer** | ISACA | OGC | ISO Board |
| **Implementation** | Information System Audit | Manage Service Level | Compliance with security standards |
| **Consultant** | Accounting Company, IT Consulting Company | IT Consulting Company | IT Consulting Company, Security Company, Network Consultant |

**Table 2: Overview of COBIT, ITIL and ISO/IEC 27002 (Priandoyo, 2008)**

"COBIT provides best practices and tools for monitoring and mapping IT processes while ITIL aims to map IT service level management and ISO 27002 provides guidelines for implementing a standardized information security framework." (Năstase, 2009)

### 2.4.2. Interconnecting of the three reference models

The three reference model can be combined if a single reference model does not fit into the organisations processes. But this is a complex venture which has been already the subject of many researches at worldwide level with the goal of obtaining a harmony between the reference models in order to simplify the mapping of IT standards in organisations (Greenfield, 2007).

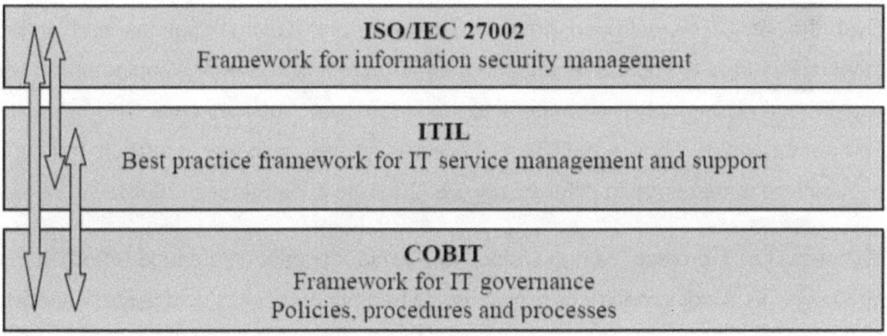


**Figure 5: Interconnection the standards (Năstase, 2009)**

Specific practices and standards such as ITIL and ISO/IEC 27002 cover selective areas and both can be mapped to the COBIT framework. Therefore a providing hierarchy of guidance materials is given (Năstase, 2009).

Before using a reference model, the needs and requirements in an organisation must be clear to choose the right IT best practice standards. This is a time consuming challenge and not every company has the time to discover all the necessary issues for a decision.

On the other hand a lot of developed tools for IT management issue are developed with the support of a specific reference model and therefore a guideline to one of the reference model is given out of the box. It can be an advantage if the reference model as well as the tool fits to an organisation but it can be a disadvantage if one of them does not fit.

## 2.5. Definition of success factors in IT projects

The understanding of the role of the IT in businesses and management as changed in recent years and therefore the understanding about the function of controlling IT and information systems (IS). Where in the past IT was seen as a cost factor, nowadays is seen as a management value and benefit (Tiemeyer, 2011).

Over the years, experienced project managers, project organisations and project researchers tried to find out at what time an IT project is successful implemented and could not commonly agreed into a definition of success (Thomas & Fernández, 2008). Thus, a definition of success as well as failure is difficult and could have different meanings to different people (Thomas & Fernández, 2008).

"Success, for IT projects, is not a 'black and white' concept (Wateridge, 1998). It can be viewed as a combination of project implementation success and system success (Espinosa et. al., 2006). Systems success can be separated into three levels: technical development, deployment to the user and delivery of business benefits (Ballantine et. al., 1996) or treated as a four-dimension construct consisting of the success of development process, success of the use process, quality of product, and impact on the organization (Saarinen, 1996)." (Thomas & Fernández, 2008)

This literature offers a lot of conceptual and different definitions of success but all agreed to one success factor which is the delivery of benefits and is it widely agreed that it depends strongly on the business sector were the company active as well as on the company themselves.

A number of companies are using the wrong measurement method key performance indicators (KPI) and the reason is that very few of them have explored what a KPI actually is (Parmenter, 2010). Parmenter (2010) offers five types for performance measurement:

1. Key result indicators (KRI) tell how something is done in a perspective or critical success factor.
2. Result indicators (RI) are telling what is done.
3. Performance indicators (PI) are telling what is to do.
4. KPI's are telling what is to do to increase the performance dramatically.

## 2.6. Hypotheses

The previous discussions on proper success factor analysis have resulted into five hypotheses:

H1: Mainly the realised human resource change management issues were able to lead to the measureable project success for the second attempt of the IT change and release management application implementation.(Based on chapter 2.2 and 2.3)

H2: The second attempt of the workflow-based CCMDB IT change and release management application implementation with their redesigned and optimised processes has a measureable higher success compared to the first attempt to introduce the CCMDBIT change and release management application as well the forerunner of the non-workflow-based Wikie IT change management method. (Based on chapter 2.4 and 2.5)

H3: Optimised and transparent process designing, inclusive the support of an IT reference model, leads to a lower resistance of the end user against the IT change and release management application.(Based on chapter 2.3, 2.4 and 2.5)

H4: The IT change management processes of the ITIL® reference model does always fit for the organisation without any modifications.(Based on chapter 2.5)

H5: Further success factors exist for an IT change and release management application implementation which are not described in the literature.

# 3. Empirical Research Methodology

The following section outlines the applied research methodology.

It is very crucial to decide on the right research method before conducting the data collection to answer the research questions. This chapter will explain the research approaches and outlines the advantages and disadvantages of the primary data. Moreover it will go further into the details of sampling, designing and analysing the questionnaire.

## 3.1. Research approaches

This present book reflects the positivist research theory as it is described by Saunders et al. (2009) which requires objective, rational and scientific research methods. The research chain is well-considerably designed and leaves no room for personal judgements and no interferences are allowed during the research processes. Therefore the data collection for the present research study should be quantifiable and repeatable at any time.

### 3.1.1. Interpretivsm vs. realism

It is widely agreed that there does not exist a scientific way in studying the social world. This means that the present research study can also be seen from the realism philosophy approach and includes as well as views from the interpretivist philosophers who like to interpret findings based on direct communication than to statically analyse the observed data.

### 3.1.2. Deductive vs. inductive research

The present research study is a positivist approach, which is closely related to the deductive research strategy (Saunders et al., 2009) which is the opposite if the inductive approach. The deductive approach is described as a logical derivation of a particular from a general. It is widely agreed that a deductive study contains four typical steps:

1. Identify the hypothesis to be tested (see chapter 2.6)
2. Generate prediction from the hypothesis(for human issues resources issues only partially applied in the present research study)
3. Use experiments to check whether predictions are correct (see chapter 3.1.3 and 3.2)
4. Analysing of the findings and decision if the hypothesises need to be modified (see chapter 4 and 5)

The inductive research has difficulties because it contains always uncertainty about the trueness of the results. Inductive inferences are always uncertain conclusions because they are from the basis of the observed and actually leave logic unequivocal. This problem of induction called weakness of inductive inference has for centuries been an important to epistemology and methodology. The induction problem is still unsolved; i.e.it can not formally specify how a safe conclusion can be done on the basis of unobserved topics and unknown future events without practicing fortune-telling (Bortz & Döring, 2006). The inductive method in this case is not targeted at producing any results for the present research study and is therefore not applied.

To modify the existing theory the definitions on the research questions must be clearly outlined and the population have to be selected carefully. The same is valid for the statistical analysis inclusive the usage of the tool. The present research study based on the deductive approach and the population and sampling selection is presented in chapter 3.1.3.

#### *3.1.2.1. Information gathering*

Information was gathered from books from a University of Cologne and Amazon purchases. Further researches were done with the help of the internet-based search engine Google Scholar but mainly with the help of MyAthens. The key words I used for the finding the right sources were e.g. IT change management, ITIL change management, introduction of MIS, human resource change management and many more.

#### *3.1.2.2. Data gathering*

Asking other companies for their success factors was a challenging venture, because there were not willing to offer the internal data for unknown reasons. Only one company gave a short insight in their success factors but it was not allowed to use the data for the present research study.

On the other hand the questionnaire with the employees and the interview with the managers of the expertise team gave a helpful insight into the success factors and all were interested to get the results of the present research study.

### 3.1.3. Quantitative vs. Qualitative Research approach

Quantitative research aims to objective findings, the best are obtained by observation and measuremental experimental studies. The aim of quantitative research is to provide generalized explanations and generally applicable laws. It should be "phenomena are determined in their frequency and distribution" (Flick et al., 1995). In quantitative research the part of the subjective aspects of the researcher and "researched" largely ignored.

The quantitative research method for the present research study is selected because it is the best method to test the results against a hypothesis.

For the quantitative research a sample survey is used because it can easily examine a large number of people for statistically reliable results without producing psychological influences and time pressure on the respondents.

On the other hand a sample survey has the challenge of not getting the whole rate of return and has the problem that the largest possible numbers of cases are needed. Individual specifics are neglected in favour of general trends (Adler, 2010).

Questionnaires were used for the empirical research and they are in the German language which is the standard language for the organisation. The advantages for the research are:

- Accurately quantifiable results
- Identification of possible statistical relationships
- Ability to analyse a large sample and thus obtain representative results
- High external validity from a large sample
- Greater objectivity and comparability of results

Flick (2002) describes the qualitative method as a scientific method that wishes to obtain answers on specific questions which are regarded as universally valid and this aim follows up the present research study which should be presented in chapter 5.

The sample survey is not flexible during the investigation by the standardisation of the examination situation, the questions have already been set, and no individual approach is possible to the test subjects. Moreover it is impossible to find out the reasons for the answers of the respondents and to reduce this issue the survey contains some open questions to determine causes. But to include open questions is not a guarantee of receiving any suggestion for reasons or improvements.

In order to input suggestions the present research study is supplemented with an interview which is a qualitative research method. As Bechhofer and Paterson (2000) stated a combination of a qualitative and a quantitative research leads to a better result as well as to a deeper understanding and this research study follows up this combination.

The target of the qualitative research is to understand the technical problems and to get the emotional reactions of the interview partners in the form of gestures. The face to face interview was a useful decision for this research because it is a problem orientated topic that is too difficult to get a comprehensive insight of the success factors and to discuss in depth the reasons of failure and suggestions of improvement only in a questionnaire. A depth quality of data is important because of having a multitude of processes and technical terms which can be clarified during the interview to come to a common denominator.

Although the interview is difficult to evaluate during the interview further enquiries from the interviewer were given. The requirements for the qualifications of the interviewer / observer are quite high; the quality of the data is to some extent dependent on it, but this is the method given in the present research study.

The analysis of an interview is relatively complex because that from the answers numerical quantities cannot be derived. Background knowledge and a deep understanding of the interviewer / observer must exist to gain this result.

For this a second supplement and therefore the third source implemented into the present research study is the personal observation of the author. The author has been working for three years in the ITSM department and therefore was able to witness the development as well as to collect some reactions of the users during this time. The observations are also a kind of qualitative research and have the following advantages:

- Flexible application of the method, as method adapts to the investigation and not vice versa
- The openness of the approach makes it possible to discover new, previously unknown facts
- Since the participants have no rules, you get more honest and complete information on the subjective view of the interlocutor
- The focus is determined by the participant, thus it is particularly relevant for the participants on the issues
- With personal interaction it is possible to obtain background information and to eliminate ambiguities

- Higher content validity is possible due to unpredetermined procedure and open questioning shows greater subjectivity of results

This method is difficult to use because the observation could be prejudiced which could have a tremendous impact on the results and therefore on the conclusions and recommendations. The observation is for the present research study reflected a subordinated topic but helps to orchestrate the information's and results.

#### *3.1.3.1. Structure of the employee questionnaire*

The questionnaire starts with a short instruction on the first page proceeds to the second page with the questions and ends on the third page with thanks. The second page contains in sum 20 questions which are split into three parts.

- Part 1: Change Management success factors issues
    - 11 questions: 10 to selection and 1 open text
- Part 2: IT change management process issues
    - 7 questions: 4 to select and 3 open text
- Part 3: Demographical issues
    - 2 questions: 2 to select

In some of the questions are further explanations added to make sure that a question and therefore the answers are made clear. Before starting the survey the questionnaire was tested by colleagues, fellow students and selected friends which are working in the IT business.

#### *3.1.3.2. Structure of the employee interview*

The interview starts with a short instruction and with a short review of the questionnaire. Like the questionnaire the interview was split into three parts and the open text questions were discussed beforehand. The reason for this is that the open text questions were closely related to the previous questions.

- Part 1: Change Management success factors issues
    - Two questions to be discussed
- Part 2: IT change management process issues
    - Six questions to be discussed
- Part 3: Demographical issues
    - No further questions to be discussed

No pre-testing for the interview was necessary.

Three types of the interview exists

- Structured
- Unstructured
- Semi-structured / semi-standardised

For the interview the semi-structured type was selected because the advantage that the interviewee will be given more room for own formulations. Therefore, the semi-standardised interview goes into more depth than the standard, and it may be deviated from the predetermined interview guide.

### 3.2. Population and Sampling

A population is the whole set of actions or people or objects which is available for a research (Sekaran, 2003) and a sample is portion of the population in which the researcher wants to undertake the investigations. It must be clear that a sample size represents the population and therefore the sample selection has to be done deliberate.

### 3.2.1. Sampling of the employee questionnaire

The target population for this research study was selected by identifying all IT change and release management users which are currently working with the system. Therefore, the CCMDB application was elected to get the sample size with a result of 134 users.

| **Organisational level** | **Sample size** |
|---|---|
| Anonym-IT GmbH – Department Root | 2 |
| Anonym-IT GmbH – Department A | 5 |
| Anonym-IT GmbH – Department B | 57 |
| Anonym-IT GmbH – Department C | 14 |
| Anonym-IT GmbH – Department D | 1 |
| Anonym-IT GmbH – Department E | 46 |
| Anonym-IT GmbH – Department F | 9 |
| Anonym-IT GmbH – Department G | - |
| **Total** | **134** |

**Table 3: Questionnaire Sample Size(own diagram)**

No random selection method was necessary to apply because every 134 employees of the total target population could contacted for the research. The definition of the portion of the population is excluded through the fact that no more employees had an insight on this empirical research topic.

The sample size of 134 employees got an invitation via email inside of the organisation with a link to an external questionnaire website. The link to the questionnaire are not personalised because of the fact that the respondents should feel free to give their individual answers. Additionally the employees were able to decide the timeframe in which to fill-out the questionnaire themselves.

### 3.2.2. Sampling of the employee interview

The face to face interview was done after the questionnaire with the managers of the expertise team of every specialised department and counted in total 12 people. The people were selected because of their overall knowledge of IT-based area of expertise as well as being able to evaluate the different behaviours of their colleagues.

A minimum of 10 to 20 persons are manageable for an interview which also makes sure that a qualitative research is given (Kornmeier, 2007). The bases for the interview are the open questions from the questionnaire. The managers of the expertise team got an MS-Outlook invitation which was sent over the company email account and invitees had to accept or reject the interview appointment.

### 3.3. Data Analysis

Primary data from the questionnaire and the interviews was collected for analysis. The questionnaire was analysed with the help of graphical charts. The graphical visualisation had the advantage that the charts can better explore, interpret as well understand the data with regard to the validity of the hypotheses.

The following techniques are used for chapter 5 for the data analysis:

- *Bar charts* to illustrate frequencies of categories
- *Line graphs* to examine trends over time
- *Pie charts* to show relative proportions

The analysis of the data themselves was made with the statistical tools from the website Q-Set.de and complemented with the statistical as well as graphical functions of the MS-Excel application.

### 3.4. Reliability

Reliability is defined as getting of comparable results or repeating the same in statistical trials. The sample of the present study is able to turn statements into a generalised conclusion for the IT business in a retailing industry in Germany. The present study can be reproduced in other industry segments or countries to enlarge the radius of the validity.

### 3.5. Limitations

The present research study contains some limitations which should be mention at this point.

To test the hypothesis a mixture of interviews and questionnaire was set. A mixture of both methods can be disadvantage because of having a time-consuming data collection as well as analyses. This circumstance can lead to compressed result.

A further limitation could appear that the respondents of the questionnaire could be in a bad mood or could have a prejudice of the topic and did not answer the questions truthfully. The interviewee could be cautious in answering because of fearing the result of being too honest. This can happen if the interview partner is very depend on the job or does not want to lose his / her position.

On the other hand the ITIL® reference model cannot be clear for everybody or other lack of knowledge can influence the results. If so, a higher data quality can be reached after training or after a long-term usage of the IT change and release management application of all the employees. With a deeper understanding of the process issues the results can move completely into another direction and therefore it is hard to forecast if the present research is repeatable exactly in this way in the future.

# 4. Presentation and analysis of data

After describing the best method of getting appropriate data for the research questions in the previous chapter, the results of the research will be presented and explained in the present chapter.

## 4.1. Demographical statistic

The demographical statistic for the age is split into the questionnaire respondents as well as into the interview partners.

### 4.1.1. Questionnaire

As it can be seen in Figure 6 is the average age of the questionnaire respondents is lying with 63 per cent between 41 and 55 years.

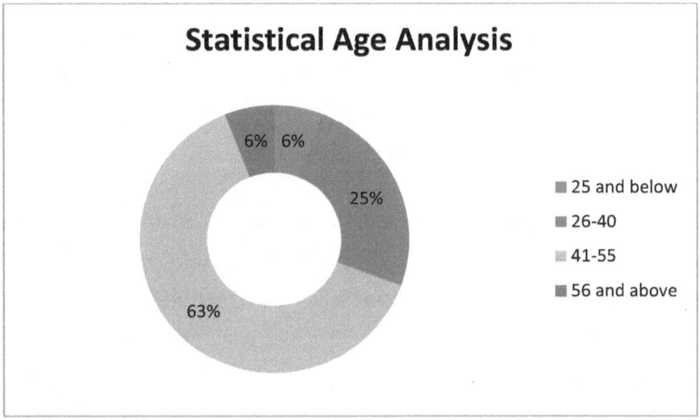


**Figure 6: Statistical Age Analysis (own diagram)**

### 4.1.2. Interview

As it can be seen in Figure 7 the average age of the questionnaire respondents is approximately a 50 per cent division between 41 and 55 years of age.

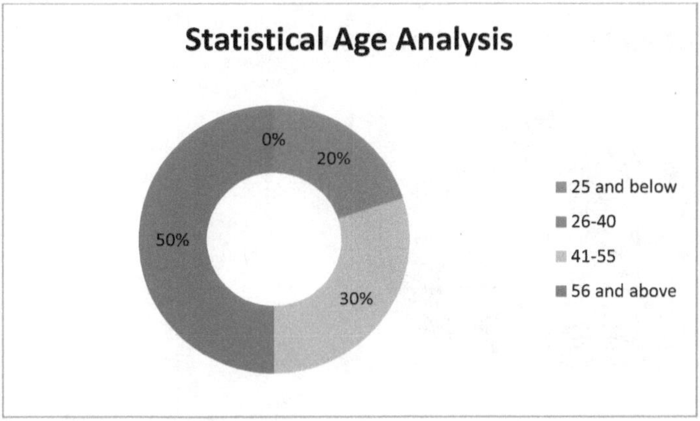


**Figure 7: Statistical Age Analysis (own diagram)**

## 4.2. Results of questionnaire

134 persons received the questionnaire and 85 of them answered completely all the 20 questions of the survey. This is a feedback quote of nearly 63 per cent which exceed the expectation given in the empirical research literature.

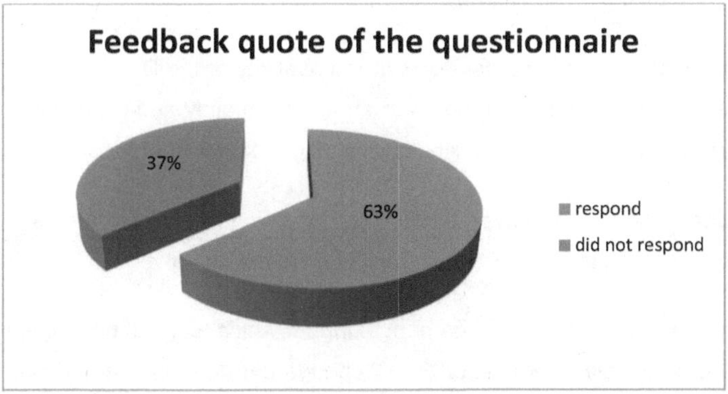


**Figure 8: Feedback quote of the questionnaire (own diagram)**

### 4.2.1. Need of an IT Change Management

All of the respondents were familiar with the IT change and release management issues and 80 of 85 persons have the opinion that a usage of it is needed.

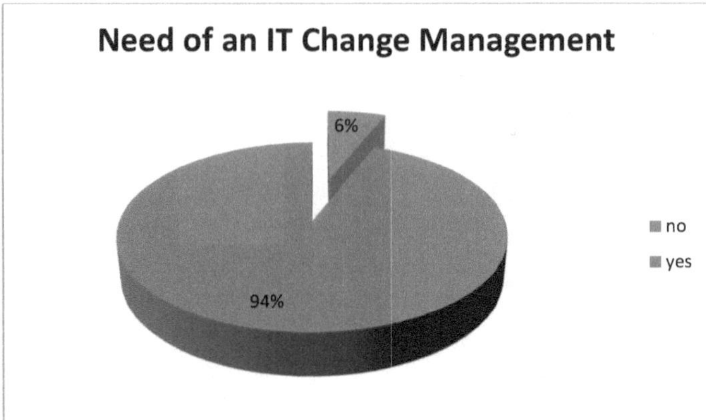


**Figure 9: Need of an IT Change Management (own diagram)**

### 4.2.2. General Success Factor Analysis

To discover the importance of the success factors the respondents had to order the factors on a scale from 1 to 12. The value 1 is the most important factor and therefore the shorter the bar the important is this factor. The following figure reflects the cumulative average of all the given answers.

The most important factor saw the respondents in the usability of the IT system. The IT change and release management application should be mainly self-explained in the handling inclusive to have a good stability as well as good performance.

The second important factor is to have standardised and transparent processes. A uniform working of every IT employee in the organisation is the aim of all.

The third important factor is the management support which should be present continuously during the whole operation of the IT change and release management application and during the whole organisation.

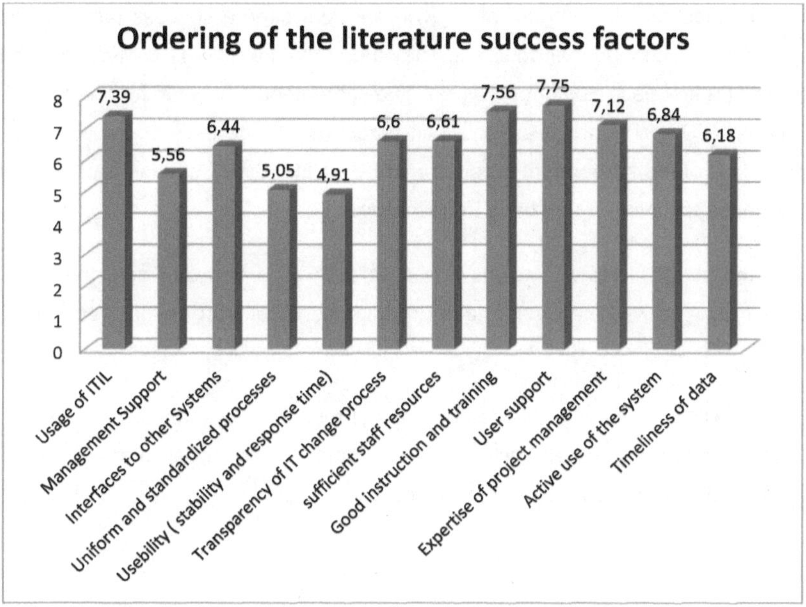


**Figure 10: Ordering of the literature success factors (own diagram)**

### 4.2.3. Additional success factor analysis

In this open question the respondents had to give their opinions on additional factors which could lead to success for the IT change and release management application implementation.

13 respondents did not suggest any additional success factors and therefore 72 answers were left to analyse. 39 answers dealt with the suggestion that the IT change and release management application have to be actively used by everyone without exception.

14 answers dealt with the management support issues. Although it was one success factor in the question in chapter 4.2.2 the respondents mentioned it again in the present question. They argued that is necessary for the full management support for the IT change and release management application and that is clear for every employee of the organisation.

The third suggestion with a count of 8 given answers sees a success factor in the simplicity of the IT change management. They argued that a RfC / IT change must be performed at a fast pace does not drag on. The same should be valid for the authorisation of the RfC's / IT changes. For a fast processing in the daily operations environment some of the respondents argued more over that the IT change and release management application would have to be intuitive.

Top 4 of the suggestions with 6 answers is to train all employees onto the ITIL® reference model as well as to undertake an ITIL® certification for every department manager.

Top 5 deals with a score of 5 that more personal resources are needed because of having an overload of work and without enough time it is not possible to use the IT change and release management application.

### 4.2.4. Adoption of ITIL® process success factors for RfC and IT change

Every change of an IT component starts with a RfC in the ITIL® reference model before it becomes an IT change and the respondents should answer if this process can be adopted one to one.

58 respondents answered with a yes and 27 respondents have the opinion that an adoption is not realisable.

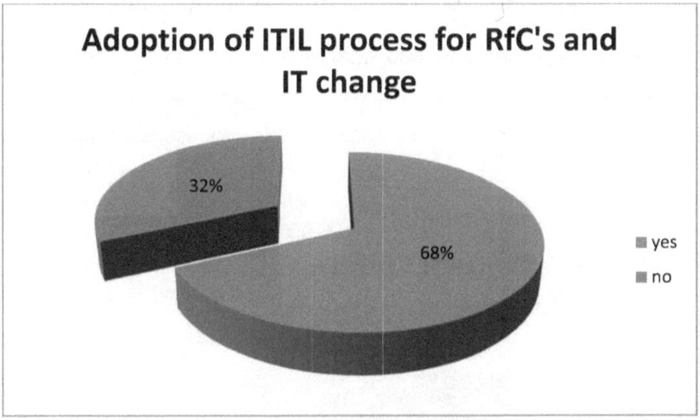


**Figure 11: Adoption of ITIL® process for RfC's (own figure)**

### 4.2.5. Justification the adoption of ITIL® process for RfC and IT change

In this open question the respondents had to justify their answer for the RfC / IT change process which was given in previous question.

27 employees answered in question in chapter 4.2.4 with no and one of them did not give a comment in the present question. 26 answers were left to analyse. Nearly 2/3 of the given answers are dealing with a too complicated and too complex process chain. For this, they further, argued that it is a time-consuming process which needs more employee resources or less a work overload on the existing employees.

58 respondents answered in question in chapter 4.2.4 with yes and 14 of them give not an additional comment in the present question. 44 answers were left to analyse.

Nearly 2/3 of the 44 given answers are dealing with the argument that a defined process chain of the ITIL® reference model makes sense and is needed. Their commented furthermore that it is important to follow the ITIL® process chain approach because of transparency and because the ITIL® process is well defined and comprehensible in books and in the internet.

### 4.2.6. ITIL® process success factors of the RfC / change authorisation

As it is described in the literature (see appendix chapter 7.3) the RfC and the change has to be authorised from a central person which has the role of the change manager. The present question wants to know the estimation if this process is useful for the organisation.

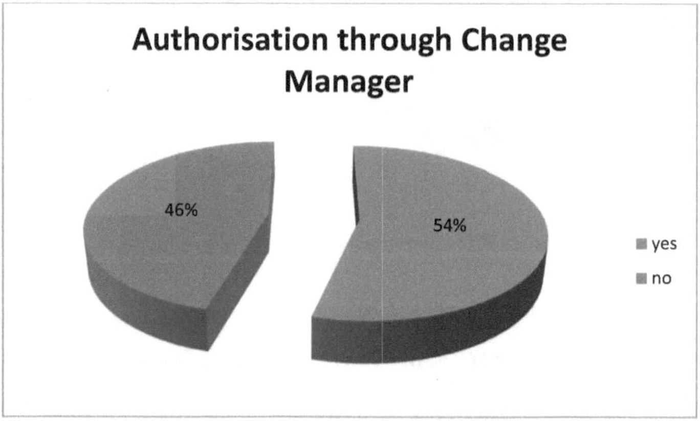


**Figure 12: Authorisation through Change Manager (own diagram)**

### 4.2.7. Justification of the RfC / change authorisation

In this open question the respondents have to justify their selected answer of the previous question for the RfC / change authorisation process.

39 respondents answered in question of the chapter 4.2.6 with a no and argued consistently throughout that one person is not able to assess all the IT changes with their consequences as well as to understand all the technical components inclusive their relationships. 1/3 of the respondents argued furthermore that the central change manager is not 24 hours available and therefore the authorisation process could be become unnecessary lengthily.

With a yes answered 46 respondents in the present question and 8 of them did not commented any suggestion. Therefore 38 answers were left to analyse. Their argued that a central person must have an overview of all the IT changes inside of the organisation and can coordinate the IT changes if problems are occurring.

### 4.2.8. Personal ITIL® benefits

The respondents were asked in the present question which personal benefits there have from the usage of the ITIL® reference model. Multiple answers were possible.

The highest benefit with 64 answers is to standardise the process followed by the consistent use of the terminology as well as followed by the definition of issues respectively areas of expertise and responsibilities.

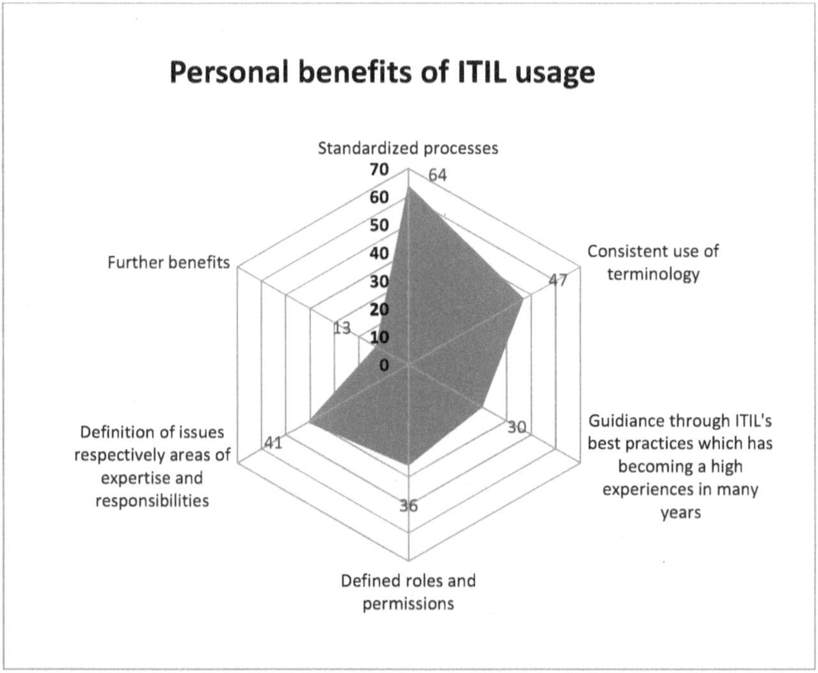


**Figure 13: Personal benefits of ITIL® usage (own diagram)**

## 4.3. Results of the interview

Like mentioned in chapter 3.1.3 and 3.2 an interview was undertaken to review the open text question inclusive to the previous questions of chapter 4.2.

### 4.3.1. Additional success factor analysis of question 4.2.3

The result of the interviews with the managers of the expertise team did not offer any more success factors which were given in the answers of the question.

### 4.3.2. Justification the adoption of ITIL® process for RfC and IT change of question 4.2.5

The present question during the interviews with the manager of the expertise team challenged the answers given in chapter 4.2.5. Five of the ten managers answered with and argued that the process workflow is difficult to grasp and too time-consuming to practice it in the daily operational business unit.

The other five managers of the expertise team agreed hesitantly initially into an adoption of the ITIL® process for the RfC and IT change process. After the question if they understood the process it was soon clear that the interviewer had to explain the ITIL® process. After the explanation of the process six of seven interview partner could not agree into the RfC process anymore. They argued like the other five managers of the expertise team that is too difficult to implement as well as too time-consuming for the AB operational unit.

### 4.3.3. Justification of the RfC / change authorisation of question 4.2.7

The present question challenges the manager of the expert team with the question of chapter 4.2.6 and 4.3.2.

After some explanations and discussions 80 per cent of the interview partners have had the opinion that a combination of the authorisation process should be implemented. A combination of a technical authorisation as well of an organisational authorisation should be implementing. They argued moreover that the process should be simple and easy in the usage without having further time-consuming issues in the daily operational work.

### 4.3.4. Additional issues of the interview

Four of the interview partners argued that they wanted to open more IT changes but have not the resources to do so. They said that they have a work overload and therefore not enough time to open an IT change.

Five of the interview partners asked if the IT change and release management application will have a rollout into the other department units outside from AB and argued that a just a usage of the system in the whole organisation should be given to have an overall improvement for the Anonym-IT GmbH.

The interview offered additionally that nearly 70 per cent of the employees are missing a knowledge management system for the IT change and release management application. They criticised that the transparent processes need a platform in order to document the job tasks themselves.

Every interview partner mentioned that the incident and problem management application would have to be integrated into the CCMDB solution and argued that it should be realised in developing an overall management tool for the IT environment.

# 5. Conclusions and recommendations

The present chapter offers conclusions and recommendations as well as theoretical implication based on the results which were presented as well as analysed in chapter 4. The conclusions are starting with two general conclusions of the demographical statistic and the need of the IT change and release management application. Then comes the conclusion for each of the four hypothesises. The recommendations are split into managerial recommendation for the Anonym-IT GmbH and for other organisations. Finally the theoretical implications are worked out.

## 5.1. Conclusion of the need of the IT change and release management

Chapter 4.2.1 offers that 94 per cent of the employees have the opinion that in IT change and release management is needed as well is necessary. This fact is the best fundamental basis for every IT change and release management application implementation so that the following improvements should help to steer the MIS into an overall success.

## 5.2. Conclusion of the demographical statistic

At the beginning of the present chapter 5 a short overview of the respondents is given. Chapter 4.1 figured out that 88 per cent of the respondents are between the age 26 and 55. The age of the interview partners which are the managers of the expertise team are higher with quote of 80 per cent between 41 till to the retirement age. Over 2/3 of them have a job tenure of longer than 10 years. The ages and seniority of the respondents and interview partners reflected that the given answers in the questionnaire can be seen as a good data basis because of having long time experiences in the IT business. Therefore a representative conclusion and recommendation should be given in the present chapter.

### 5.3. Conclusions of the hypothesises

The conclusion interprets the results of the questionnaire and the interviews for each hypothesis. Every hypothesis will be analysed for validation and if there exist a need to be modified.

#### 5.3.1. Hypothesis 1

*Mainly the realised human resource change management issues were able to lead to the measureable project success for the second attempt of the IT change and release management application implementation.*

Hypothesis 1 is not valid in that point that just the human resource change management issues lead to a successful IT change and release management application implementation.

The deployment of change agents which are the managers of expertise team and the restructure of the department unit AB led to a higher success rate as compared to the first roll out of the IT change and release management application, because the change agents have yearly target agreements where the topic is now a goal for them.

The managers as well for every department in the department unit AB received the topic on their yearly target agreement. Furthermore the managers got an explanation of the purpose and mission of the IT change and release management application.

Additionally, the managers introduced the role of a process sponsor for the IT change and release management application which has the target that every manager has to support the application with all the available resources.

Interestingly, the end users argued that the main success factors are the uniformed processes as well the usability of the IT change and release management application and just after this both issues the management support is mentioned.

General it can be said that the success factors given in the human resource change management literature is able to support an introduction of an IT change and release management application but the application themselves has also to comply with their success factors. Both issues are therefore complementary.

Hypothesis testing based on the findings described in 4.2.2 to 4.2.3 and 4.3.1.

### 5.3.2. Hypothesis 2

*The second attempt of the workflow-based CCMDB IT change and release management application implementation with their redesigned and optimised processes has a measureable higher success compared to the first attempt to introduce the CCMDB IT change and release management application as well the forerunner of the non-workflow-based Wikie IT change management method.*

Hypothesis 2 is valid that the process orientated IT change and release management application could reach a higher success.

The non-process IT change management method names Wikie started in October 2006 till to end of January 2012 which were 66 month and contains a sum of 4335 changes. Round about 66 IT changes were opened in a month in the non-process IT change management website.

The first CCMDB IT change and release management application implementation were stopped after 12 IT changes over the period of two months. Just 6 of 14 end users used the application and the average opened IT changes per month are only 6.

The second implementation of the CCMDB IT change and release management application offers since January a value over 436 IT changes which has in average of 145 IT changes per month. This is more than a duplication which can therefore be defined as a success.

Depending of the process orientated workflow the CCMDB IT change and release management application 12 IT changes could prevent a modification on an IT system which was blocked during the frozen zone period.

Also the end user usage of the application increased. An analysis of the end user who opens an IT change increased from 62 to 73 compared between the IT change management applications.

On top the end user feedback where the users explained that they are for the first time satisfied with the new IT change and release management application and announced to work more intensively with this in the future.

Hypothesis testing based on the findings described in 4.3.4 and on the analysing of the three IT change management environments with a reporting tool. Additional the testing based on observation during periodic meetings and getting feedback during these appointments.

### 5.3.3. Hypothesis 3

*Optimised and transparent process designing leads to a lower resistance of the end user against the IT change and release management application.*

The hypothesis 3 is valid that the transparency of processes let the employee's lower resist against the IT change and release management application.

The data analysis offers that to have transparent processes the chance is higher for the end users to understand the dependencies of their work as well as to understand the work of their colleagues. Their see it as an advantage to improve their own work and therefore for the whole organisation.

The reason for this opinion is that in the past the way of working was not clear for everybody to grasp especially for the new employees who had recently entered the organisation. For them it is always difficult to get the right contact person as well as the right information for their own work and becoming is connected with a time consuming venture.

Hypothesis testing based on the findings described in 4.2.2 to 4.2.3 and 4.3.1.

### 5.3.4. Hypothesis 4

*The IT change management process of the ITIL® reference model does always fit for the organisation without a modification.*

The hypothesis 4 is valid in that point that the ITIL® reference model does fit for any organisation even if a customization is necessary or a combination with other reference models like in chapter 2.4.2 suggested can be realised.

The ITIL® reference model does fit for the organisation especially if no reference model or other comparable process designs are used before. The usage of the ITIL® reference model is able to transfer the organisation to standardised processes working without to develop in a self-managed way. This method saves time and the process transparency it given because the processes can easily be checked on various internet websites.

The ITIL® reference model can therefore lead as a profound guideline to compare the processes of the organisation against the model. The gaps between the requirements of the organisation and the ITIL® reference model can be redesigned to improve the process issues.

The fourth hypothesis testing based on the findings described in 4.2.1 to 4.2.2 and 4.3.2 to 4.3.3.

### 5.3.5. Hypothesis 5

*Further success factors exist for an IT change and release management application implementation which are not described in the literature.*

The hypothesis 5 is valid in that point that further success factors could be found.

Further success factor could be found for the usability of an IT change and release management application in that way that it works stable and have a high respond time. Performance issues as a success factor could not be found in the literature.

Another success factor could be found to improve the process issues. The formal RfC can be skipped and the entry point for the request can be directly the IT change form.

A third success factor with a high quality improvement could be found if the authorisation process is done by a technical involved employee. The ITIL® reference model suggests a central person which has normally a superficial understanding for all the IT issues. It is important to integrate a technical knowledge able employee in the process so that the authorisation process can to be implemented with a selected employee of every expertise.

The fifth hypothesis testing based on the findings described 4.2.2 to 4.2.7 and 4.3.1 to 4.3.4.

## 5.4. Managerial recommendations for the organisation

The managerial recommendations are related to the outlined hypothesises in chapter 2.6. The advice should be able to improve the implementation of an IT change and release management application inside of the Anonym-IT GmbH especially for the operational department unit AB.

Relating to the human resource change management the eight step model of Kotter, which was described in chapter 2.2, could can be said that the given steps were basically realised for the second attempt of the IT change and release management application implementation. Step 4 with communication a vision and 5 with empowering others to act to on the vision of Kotter's model should be improved further to reach every employee to use the application without any exception. To explain the vision and mission only to the managers is not enough based on the given literature. Additionally the employees need the resources to use the IT change and release management application. Depending on the work overload of the employees they need a restructuring of their work or the department needs more employee resources to fulfil the requirement to use the IT change and release management application. A bonus system for key employees can support this to reach the goal.

Relating to the process issues of the IT change and release management application the success factors were mainly implemented. To optimise the processes and operational sequences the RfC of the ITIL® reference model should be skipped for the operational department AB. To begin directly with an IT change without the formal request RfC saves time as well as to simplify the processes for the employees.

To improve the quality of IT change authorisation the ITIL® change process should redesigned that not only one change manager has the responsibility for all the IT changes. The authorisation should be done by the employee who has the technical expertise to control the IT change with a regard to the content. The change manager should be a part in concert with the expert and both together are an optimised combination of technical and organisational issues.

During the second rollout phase for the CCMDB and during the questionnaire it becomes clear that the ITIL® reference model was not clear for the most of the employees. The suggestion is to train the staff into the ITIL® reference model as soon as possible. The gained knowledge and the understanding of the processes could help to increase more the acceptance as well as increases the usage of the IT change and release management application.

Beyond the standardised processes of the IT change and release management application a knowledge management system should be introduced to collect at a central place the gained knowledge of all the employees. This issue was suggested in the literature as well as a demand of the interview partners.

The department units AE, AH and AS are modifying on their self-developed applications which are on running on the IT systems of the operational AB department unit. To gain a holistic IT change and release management for the Anonym-IT GmbH the other department units should use the application as well to request an IT change. For this it can be necessary to shift the ITSM team from AB to a higher department or a team of the staff unit of the company to get more executing rights.

## 5.5. Managerial recommendations for other companies

The conclusion of the thesis is mainly based on the internal primary research data of the organisation Anonym-IT GmbH. To recommend general findings to other companies can be varied and limited. This depends on the different management and culture of every organisation as well as on the business area of the company.

In general it can be said that the other companies can take the identified best practices as a guideline which are given in the literature to improve the success of an IT change and release management implementation and has moreover to find the their own success factors like the Anonym-IT GmbH did.

For the operational IT business every company can follow the approach to skip the RfC for the request of an IT change to simplify the processes and save time.

Furthermore other companies can also follow the approach to authorise the requested IT changes form a technical knowing person instead the authorisation of a central person named the change manager.

## 5.6. Theoretical implications

This research study can make some theoretical contribution relating to the process issues.

In contrast to the literature review, the conclusion is to simplify two process workflows for an IT operational acting organisation.

Relating to the formal request (RfC) of the ITIL® reference model at the beginning of every IT change in the operational department unit can be skipped. Skipping reduces time and simplifies the process duration. The motivation lays in the fact that the RfC is just formal request without an impact of their work or without an impact to the business. Therefore the ITIL® reference model should expand in that fact that for the operational IT administrators the RfC can be skipped.

The second theoretical implication deals with the authorisation of an IT change inside of the ITIL® reference model. It should redesigned that not only one change manager has the responsibility for all the IT changes. The authorisation should be done by the employee who has the technical expertise to control the IT change with a regard to the content. The change manager should be a part beyond the expert. Therefore the ITIL® reference model should expand the possibility to set a new role between the IT change owner and the change manager.

## 6. List of references

Adler, F., (2010), [WWW] Available from: http://qsf.e-learning.imb-uni-augsburg.de/ [Accessed 07/04/12]

Anderson, D. and Ackerman Anderson, L., (2010), Beyond Change Management, 2nd edition, San Francisco, Pfeiffer, pp. 131-206

Anderson, D. and Ackerman Anderson, L., (2010), [WWW] Available from: http://media.wiley.com/assets/2258/14/PC06_TenCommonMistakes_v1_100819.pdf[ Accessed 23/03/12]

Atteran, M. and Wood, G. G., (1999) in Suhendra, E. S. and Oswari, T., (2011), *Business Process Management in Organisation: A Critical Success Factor* Journal of US-China Public Administration, Vol. 8, No. 1, pp. 110-120

Ballantine, J., Bonner, M., Levy, M., Munro, I. and Powell, P., (1996) in Thomas, G. & Fernández, W., (2008), *Success in IT projects: A matter of definition?* International Journal of Project Management, Vol. 26, pp. 733-742

Ballagun J. and Haily, V. H., (2008), Exploring Strategic Change, 3rd edition, Harlow, Prentice Hall, pp. 189-232

Bechhofer, F. & Paterson, L., (2000), Principles of Research Design in the Social Sciences, Abington, Routledge

Bortz, J. and Döring, N., (2006), Forschungsmethoden und Evalution, Heidelberg, Springer Verlag, pp. 300-301

Choi, F. C. and Chan, S. L., (1997) in Suhendra, E. S. and Oswari, T., (2011), *Business Process Management in Organisation: A Critical Success Factor* Journal of US-China Public Administration, Vol. 8, No. 1, pp. 110-120

Davenport, T.H., (1993b) in Suhendra, E. S. and Oswari, T., (2011), *Business Process Management in Organisation: A Critical Success Factor* Journal of US-China Public Administration, Vol. 8, No. 1, pp. 110-120

Espinosa, J., DeLone W. and Lee, G., (2006) in Thomas, G. & Fernández, W., (2008), *Success in IT projects: A matter of definition?* International Journal of Project Management, Vol. 26, pp. 733-742

Flick, U., von Kardorff, E., Keupp, H., von Rosenstil, L. & Wolff, S.,(1995), Handbuch Qualitative Sozialforschung, 2nd edition, Beltz, Weinheim

Flick, U., (2002), Qualitative Sozialforschung – Eine Einführung, RoRoRo, Reinbek

Früh, W., (2001), Inhaltsanalyse, 5th edition, UVK Verlagsgesellschaft, Konstanz, pp. 19- 38

Greenfield, D., (2007) in Năstase, P., (2009), [WWW] Available from: http://itsminfo.com/challenges-generated-by-the-implementation-of-the-it-standards-cobit-4-1-itil-v3-and-isoiec-27002-in-enterprises/ , [Accessed 23/03/12]

Haberberg, A. and Rieple, A, (2008), Strategic Management, Oxford, Oxford Press, pp. 686-706

Hornstein, H., (2008), in Wood, J. C. and Wood, M. C, (2011) John P. Kotter - Critical Evaluations in Business and Management, Abington, Routledge, pp. 17-27

Jacobson, I., Ericsson, M., and Jacobson, A., (1995) in Suhendra, E. S. and Oswari, T., (2011), *Business Process Management in Organisation: A Critical Success Factor* Journal of US-China Public Administration, Vol. 8, No. 1, pp. 110-120

Kornmeier, M., (2007), Wissenschaftstheorie und wissenschaftliches Arbeiten, Heidelberg, Physica

Kotter, J. P., (1996) in Wood, J. C. and Wood, M. C, (2011) John P. Kotter - Critical Evaluations in Business and Management, Abington, Routledge, pp. 17-27

Kotter, J.P. and Schlesinger, L.A., (2008), Best of HR, *Choosing Strategies for Change*, Harvard Business Review, pp. 130-139

Laudon, K. C. & Laudon, J. P., (2012), Management Information Systems, 12th edition, Harlow, Pearson, pp. 60-548

Lientz, B.P. and Rea, K.P., (2004), Breakthrough IT Change Management, Burlington, ELSEVIER, pp. 17-33

Manganelli, R. I., (1993) in Suhendra, E. S. and Oswari, T., (2011), *Business Process Management in Organisation: A Critical Success Factor* Journal of US-China Public Administration, Vol. 8, No. 1, pp. 110-120

Năstase, P., (2009), [WWW] Available from: http://itsminfo.com/challenges-generated-by-the-implementation-of-the-it-standards-cobit-4-1-itil-v3-and-isoiec-27002-in-enterprises/ , [Accessed 23/03/12]

Parmenter, D., 2010), Key Performance Indicators, 2nd edition, New Jersey, John Wiley & Son, pp. 1-27

Peltu, M., Cleeg, C. and Sell, R., (1996) in Suhendra, E. S. and Oswari, T., (2011), *Business Process Management in Organisation: A Critical Success Factor* Journal of US-China Public Administration, Vol. 8, No. 1, pp. 110-120

Priandoyo, A., (2008) in Năstase, P., (2009), [WWW] Available from: http://itsminfo.com/challenges-generated-by-the-implementation-of-the-it-standards-cobit-4-1-itil-v3-and-isoiec-27002-in-enterprises/ , [Accessed 23/03/12]

Prokesch, S.E., (2009), Organizational Behavior, *How GE Teaches Teams to Lead Change*, Harvard Business Review, pp. 1-11

Saarinen, T., (1996) in Thomas, G. & Fernández, W., (2008), *Success in IT projects: A matter of definition?* International Journal of Project Management, Vol. 26, pp. 733-742

Saunders, M., Kewis, P. & Thornhill, A., (2009), Research methods for business students, 5th edition, Edinburgh, Prentince Hall

Sekaran, U., (2003). Research methods for business, 4th edition, New Jersey, John Wiley & Sons

Suhendra, E. S. and Oswari, T., (2011), *Business Process Management in Organisation: A Critical Success Factor* Journal of US-China Public Administration, Vol. 8, No. 1, pp. 110-120

Tiemeyer, E., (2011), Handbuch IT- Management, 4th edition, Munich, Hanser, pp 8-372

Thomas, G. & Fernández, W., (2008), *Success in IT projects: A matter of definition?* International Journal of Project Management, Vol. 26, pp. 733-742

Wateridge, J., (1998) in Thomas, G. & Fernández, W., (2008), *Success in IT projects: A matter of definition?* International Journal of Project Management, Vol. 26, pp. 733-742

## 7. Appendices

Appendices are listed on the next pages.

## 7.1. The five ITIL® units

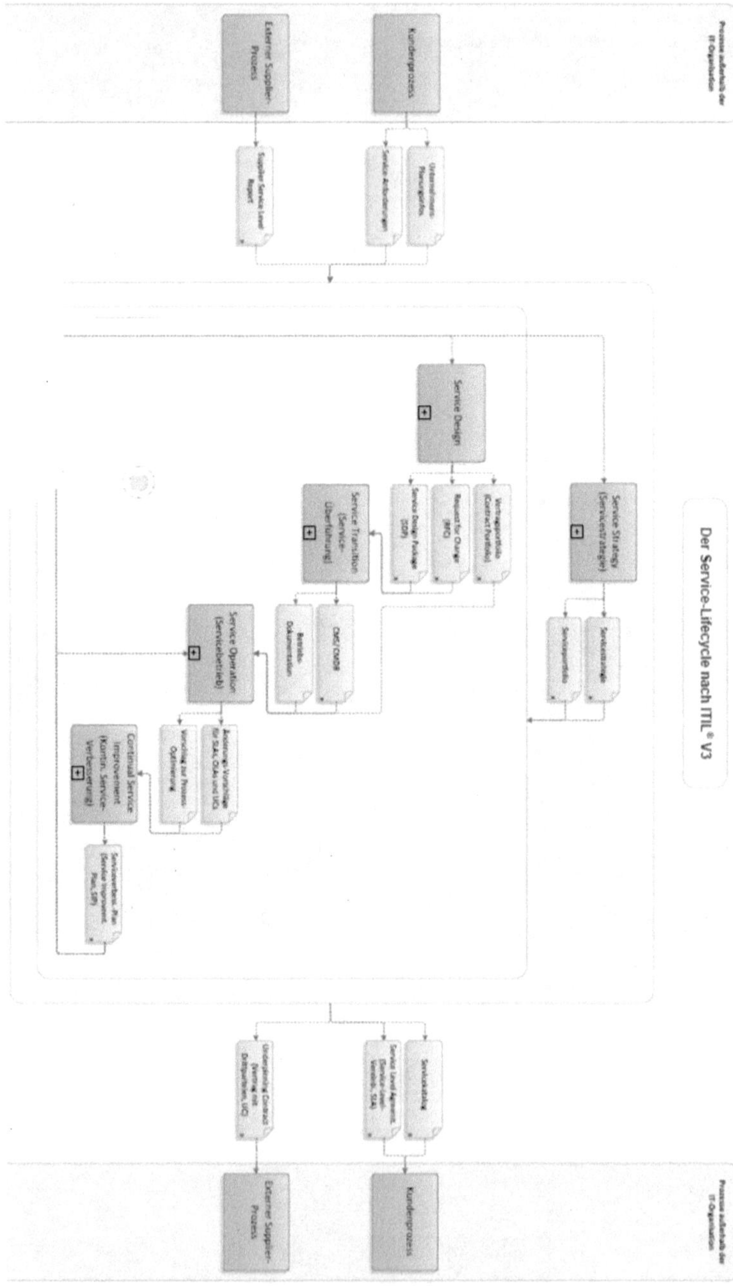

## 7.2. ITIL® Transition unit with IT change and release management

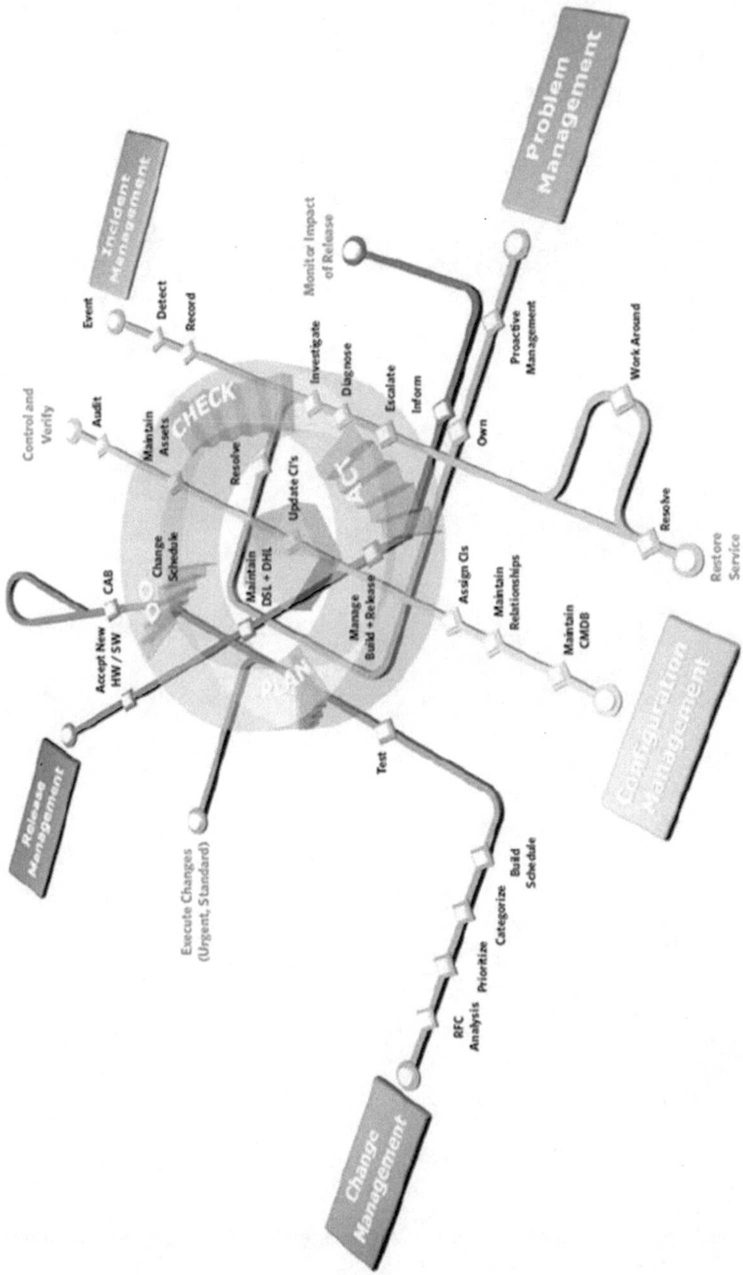

## 7.3. ITIL® IT Change Management Process Workflow

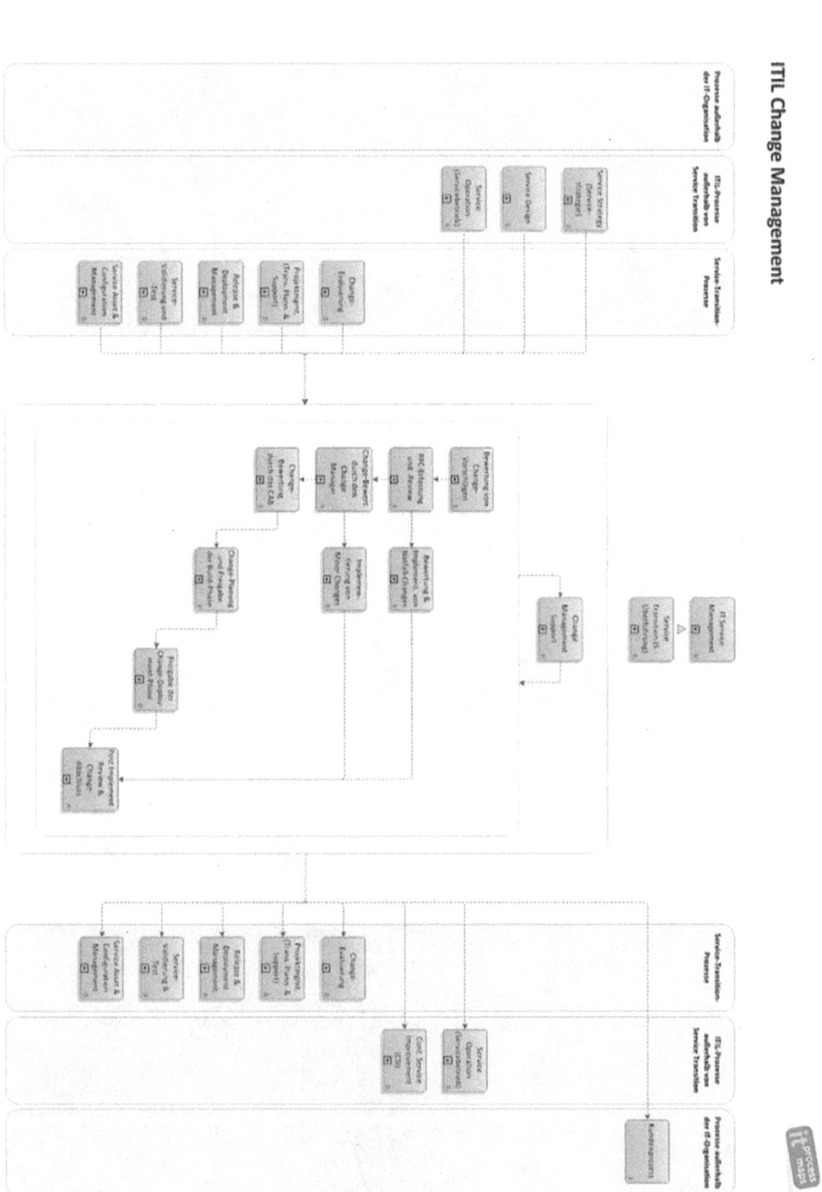


Source: http://wiki.de.it-processmaps.com/images/9/9a/Itil-change-management.jpg

www.ingramcontent.com/pod-product-compliance
Lightning Source LLC
La Vergne TN
LVHW102228300926
849160LV00005B/69